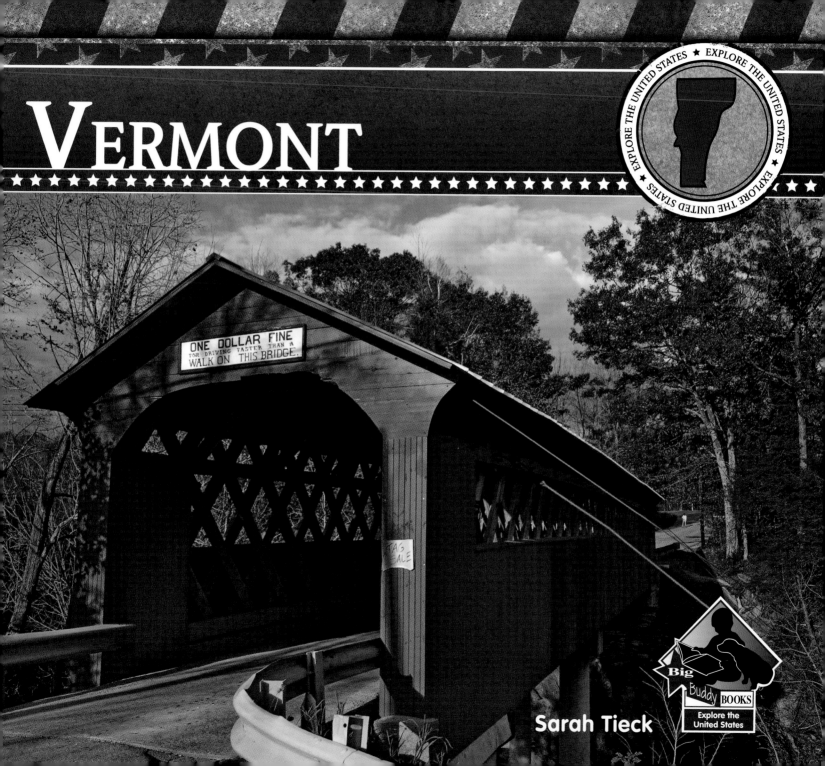

VERMONT

Explore the United States

Big Buddy BOOKS
Explore the United States

ONE DOLLAR FINE
FOR DRIVING FASTER THAN A
WALK ON THIS BRIDGE..

Sarah Tieck

VISIT US AT
www.abdopublishing.com

Published by ABDO Publishing Company, PO Box 398166, Minneapolis, MN 55439.

Printed in the United States of America, North Mankato, Minnesota.
052012
092012

PRINTED ON RECYCLED PAPER

Coordinating Series Editor: Rochelle Baltzer
Contributing Editors: Megan M. Gunderson, Marcia Zappa
Graphic Design: Adam Craven
Cover Photograph: *Shutterstock*: J. Norman Reid.
Interior Photographs/Illustrations: *Alamy*: Andre Jenny (p. 21), Tom Way (p. 27); *AP Photo*: HO (p. 23), North Wind Picture Archives via AP Images (pp. 13, 23), Mary Schwalm (p. 27); *Getty Images*: Diane Cook and Len Jenshel (p. 17), Popperfoto (p. 25); *Glow Images*: © David Frazier/Corbis (p. 19), Andre Jenny (p. 26); *iStockphoto*: ©iStockphoto.com/DenisTangneyJr (p. 9), ©iStockphoto.com/Ron_Thomas (p. 29), ©iStockphoto.com/tsm4781 (p. 11), ©iStockphoto.com/Xprtshot (p. 27); *Shutterstock*: B Brown (p. 26), Melinda Fawver (p. 30), Jeffrey M. Frank (p. 9), Stacy Funderburke (p. 5), godrick (p. 30), Philip Lange (p. 30), Stubblefield Photography (p. 30).

All population figures taken from the 2010 US census.

Library of Congress Cataloging-in-Publication Data

Tieck, Sarah, 1976-
  Vermont / Sarah Tieck.
    p. cm. -- (Explore the United States)
  ISBN 978-1-61783-384-7
  1. Vermont--Juvenile literature. I. Title.
  F49.3.T54 2013
  974.3--dc23
                        2012017233

VERMONT

Contents

One Nation 4

Vermont Up Close. 6

Important Cities 8

Vermont in History 12

Timeline 14

Across the Land 16

Earning a Living 18

Natural Wonder 20

Hometown Heroes 22

Tour Book 26

A Great State 28

Fast Facts 30

Important Words 31

Web Sites 31

Index 32

ONE NATION

The United States is a **diverse** country. It has farmland, cities, coasts, and mountains. Its people come from many different backgrounds. And, its history covers more than 200 years.

Today the country includes 50 states. Vermont is one of these states. Let's learn more about Vermont and its story!

Did You Know?

Vermont became a state on March 4, 1791. It was the fourteenth state to join the nation.

Vermont is known for the beautiful Green Mountains.

5

VERMONT UP CLOSE

The United States has four main **regions**. Vermont is in the Northeast.

Vermont has three states on its borders. New Hampshire is east. Massachusetts is south and New York is west. The country of Canada is north.

Vermont has a total area of 9,617 square miles (24,908 sq km). About 626,000 people live there. That makes it the second least-populated state!

REGIONS OF THE UNITED STATES

Legend:
- = West
- = Midwest
- = South
- = Northeast

CANADA

WASHINGTON
MONTANA
NORTH DAKOTA
MINNESOTA
VERMONT
MAINE
NEW HAMPSHIRE
OREGON
IDAHO
WYOMING
SOUTH DAKOTA
WISCONSIN
MICHIGAN
NEW YORK
MASSACHUSETTS
RHODE ISLAND
CONNECTICUT
IOWA
PENNSYLVANIA
NEW JERSEY
PACIFIC OCEAN
NEVADA
UTAH
NEBRASKA
ILLINOIS
INDIANA
OHIO
Washington DC ★
DELAWARE
MARYLAND
CALIFORNIA
COLORADO
KANSAS
MISSOURI
WEST VIRGINIA
VIRGINIA
KENTUCKY
ARIZONA
NEW MEXICO
OKLAHOMA
ARKANSAS
TENNESSEE
NORTH CAROLINA
SOUTH CAROLINA
ATLANTIC OCEAN
MISSISSIPPI
GEORGIA
TEXAS
LOUISIANA
ALABAMA
FLORIDA
GULF OF MEXICO
ALASKA
MEXICO
HAWAII
PUERTO RICO

N
W   E
S

7

IMPORTANT CITIES

Montpelier (mahnt-PEHL-yuhr) is Vermont's **capital**. It became the capital in 1805. It is the smallest state capital, with just 7,855 people.

Burlington is the largest city in the state. It is home to 42,417 people. Burlington is known for its lake and mountain landscape. The University of Vermont is in Burlington. This city is also where Ben and Jerry's ice cream was first made in 1978.

The Vermont State House was completed in 1859.

Vermont

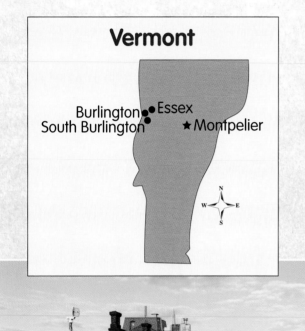

Burlington • Essex
South Burlington • ★ Montpelier

N W E S

People enjoy walking around
Burlington's downtown area.

9

Essex is the second-largest city in Vermont. It is home to 19,587 people. Essex is a historic town. It was settled in 1783.

South Burlington is the state's third-largest city. It has 17,904 people. Both Essex and South Burlington are near Burlington.

South Burlington is located on Lake Champlain.

VERMONT IN HISTORY

Vermont's history includes Native Americans, settlers, and war. Native Americans have lived in what is now Vermont for thousands of years. In 1609, the French claimed the land. In 1666, they built a **fort** on Isle La Motte in Lake Champlain.

In the 1700s, American colonists began to settle in Vermont. In 1775, many fought in the **Revolutionary War**. Two years later, Vermont became its own country. In 1791, it became part of the United States.

Vermont settlers fought in the Revolutionary War. Ethan Allen and the Green Mountain Boys were famous American soldiers from Vermont.

Timeline

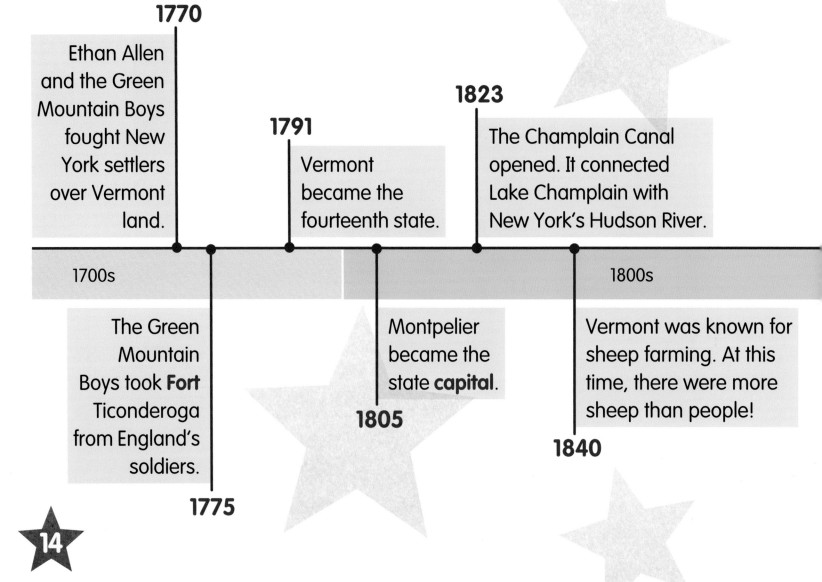

1770

Ethan Allen and the Green Mountain Boys fought New York settlers over Vermont land.

1791

Vermont became the fourteenth state.

1823

The Champlain Canal opened. It connected Lake Champlain with New York's Hudson River.

1700s

1800s

1775

The Green Mountain Boys took **Fort** Ticonderoga from England's soldiers.

1805

Montpelier became the state **capital**.

1840

Vermont was known for sheep farming. At this time, there were more sheep than people!

1927

The Winooski River and other rivers flooded. This caused the worst flooding in Vermont's history.

2011

Tropical Storm Irene caused heavy rain. Rivers flooded and ruined buildings, roads, and bridges.

1900s

2000s

Vermont became the first state to have a visitor's **bureau**.

Vermont passed the Environmental Control Law. It was one of the nation's strictest laws to keep the environment safe.

Saint Albans held its fortieth-annual Vermont Maple Festival.

1911

2006

1970

ACROSS THE LAND

Vermont has mountains, hills, valleys, lakes, and rivers. The Green Mountains are in the middle of the state. The Connecticut River forms the state's eastern border. Several smaller rivers empty into Lake Champlain in the northwest.

Many types of animals make their homes in Vermont. These include white-tailed deer, rabbits, bears, and foxes.

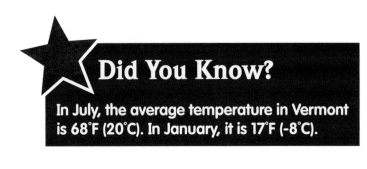

Did You Know?

In July, the average temperature in Vermont is 68°F (20°C). In January, it is 17°F (-8°C).

There are more than 70 islands in Lake Champlain. These include North Hero (*above*), Grand Isle, and Isle La Motte.

EARNING A LIVING

Vermont has many important businesses. Most people work in service jobs, such as helping visitors to the state. Others work in factories that make **electronics** or food products.

Vermont has many natural **resources**. **Granite** and marble come from the state's mines. And, milk is a leading product of Vermont's farms.

Did You Know?

Vermont is the leading producer of maple syrup in the United States.

Vermont's dairy farms produce important foods. And, they are known for their beauty.

19

NATURAL WONDER

Vermont is famous for the Green Mountains. The area is known for its beauty and history. Vermont was named for these mountains. *Vert Mont* is French for "Green Mountains."

Green Mountain National Forest has almost 400,000 acres (160,000 ha) of land. People hike, bike, ski, camp, and fish there. In the fall, many come to the area to see the trees change color.

Mount Mansfield is the state's highest
point. It is 4,393 feet (1,339 m) tall!

Hometown Heroes

Many famous people are from Vermont, including two US presidents. Chester A. Arthur was born in Fairfield in 1829. His father was a **minister**, so the family often moved. Arthur grew up in different parts of Vermont and New York. He was the twenty-first US president.

Arthur started out as vice president. He served with James A. Garfield. In 1881, Garfield was shot and killed. Arthur became president that year and served until 1885.

As president, Arthur (*above*) traveled throughout the United States. He was in New York City for the opening of the Brooklyn Bridge (*right*).

23

Calvin Coolidge was born in Plymouth in 1872. He grew up on a farm. He was the thirtieth US president.

At first, Coolidge served as vice president with Warren G. Harding. In 1923, Harding died and Coolidge became president. In 1924, Coolidge was elected for a full term. He served until 1929. The 1920s were a time of fun and financial growth for the United States.

★ **Did You Know?**

Coolidge was visiting his family's farm in Vermont when he found out Harding had died. Coolidge's father was a public official, so he gave him the oath of office.

★★★★★★★★★★★★★★★★★★★★★★★★★★★★★

Coolidge's nickname was Silent Cal. He was known for being quiet and serious.

Tour Book

Do you want to go to Vermont? If you visit the state, here are some places to go and things to do!

★ Taste

Visit a sugarhouse and try some maple syrup. When the snow melts around March, people collect maple tree sap. This is made into syrup in a sugarhouse.

★ See

Take a walk in a forest during fall. Vermont's trees are known for their beautiful colors.

★ Remember

See the home of Vermont hero Ethan Allen. The Ethan Allen Homestead Museum is in Burlington. The house was built in 1787.

★ Cheer

Go to a University of Vermont Catamounts game! The school is known for its hockey and basketball teams.

★ Discover

Visit Lake Champlain. Go for a swim. Or, learn about the 1775 capture of Fort Ticonderoga (*left*) across the lake in New York. This was an important American victory in the Revolutionary War.

A Great State

The story of Vermont is important to the United States. The people and places that make up this state offer something special to the country. Together with all the states, Vermont helps make the United States great.